THE LEGACY,
THE MAN,
THE HONORABLE
JOHN CONYERS, JR.

Preface:

All my life I have known who John Conyers Jr. is. The name John was special throughout my father's family. I was saying either Uncle Johnny, my great uncle, the congressman's father, or just John, my cousin. Come and travel down memory road with me to explore the great career and life of the Honorable Congressman John Conyers Jr. Congressman Conyers is one of the few members of the House of Representatives whose career stretches back to the civil rights era of the 1960s, and many of the key political advances of those years bore his name either as sponsor or cosponsor. Congressman Conyers has a spirit of curiosity that has led him into areas beyond civil rights, and he has worked over his long career on issues ranging from alcohol warning labels to intellectual property rights of musicians in a changing technological world. As American politics elected the first African American president, Barack Obama, Conyers continued to raise his voice in support of liberal causes and of his urban constituency. It is with great pleasure and honor that I introduce to you, my family, the Honorable John Conyers Jr.

Table of Content

In the Beginning: Background

A lifelong resident of Detroit, Michigan, John Conyers Junior was born on May 16, 1929, to John and Lucilie Conyers. John Conyers Senior was a Georgia-born laborer who dropped out of high school and came to Detroit to work at the Chrysler auto plant. He realized that black auto painters were being paid less than their white counterparts, and he made a personal protest to company president Walter P. Chrysler. The elder Conyers's union-organizing activities cost him jobs, but he eventually rose to a high position within the United Auto Workers union. John Conyers Jr., his oldest son, along with four other children, grew up in the culturally rich northwest side of Detroit.

John's passion in his high school years was music. He received a letter for playing trumpet in his high school band, and he also studied bass, piano, tenor saxophone, and trombone. Several jazz musicians who became national stars were part of Conyers's circle of friends in high school, including Sonny Stitt and Milt Jackson. "I went to Northwestern High School with Betty Carter."

"Tommy Flanagan and Kenny Burrell and I were at Wayne State University together." His favorite performer—and another friend later on—was the breaking saxophonist John Coltrane. Conyers kept an acoustic bass in one corner of his Washington office as a congressional representative, and in the 1970s, he even hosted a jazz program on Washington radio station WPFW.

The 1943 Detroit race riots, in which blacks were pulled off street-cars and attacked by white mobs, began to awaken Conyers's political consciousness, but music and school came first for a long time. Conyers breezed through high school. He often skipped classes to play pool but still graduated in 1954. There was no money for college, so he relied on his father's influence to get a job as a spot welder at a Lincoln auto plant. He became the director of his United Auto Workers local unit. Hungry for further education, he took night classes covering levels of chemistry and physics he had not reached in high school. He went on to take more night classes connected with Detroit's Wayne State University and finally enrolled there on a union-backed scholarship in the late 1940s, taking courses in civil engineering.

As the United States moved toward war in Korea, Conyers enlisted in the US Army in 1950. After serving in the National Guard (1948-1950), the United States Army (1950-54), and the United States Army Corps of Engineers in the Korean War, spending part of his officer training program at Fort Belleville in Virginia, he went to Washington to watch Congress in action and thought, "I could do that!" Reaching the rank of second lieutenant in the Army Corps of Engineers, Conyers was sent to Korea and saw combat, winning several military honors. Veterans' benefits allowed Conyers to continue his education after his army discharge, and he returned to Wayne State in 1954. He switched from engineering to pre-law and earned both his bachelor of arts (1957) and juris doctor (1958) degrees at Wayne State University. He is married to the former Monica Esters. Mr. and Mrs. Conyers have two sons, John III and Carl Edward.

Career: and what a career it's been

After joining the Detroit's Young Democratic Club, Conyers ran for the post of precinct convention delegate, inaugurating his winning political ways with a narrow victory over a rival. During this time he graduated from Wayne State in 1957 and finished a law degree at the same school the following year, passing the bar exam and cofounding the law firm of Conyers, Bell, and Townsend soon after that.

An accident of geography helped rekindle Conyers's political ambitions: his law office was in the same building as that of veteran Michigan US Representative John Dingell, who as of 2005 was the only lawmaker with more seniority than Conyers. The arrangement was beneficial from a business standpoint, as people involved in landlord-tenant disputes filtered into Conyers's office. Conyers took the chance to broaden his circle of political contacts, working in Dingell's office from 1959 to 1961 and snaring a political appointment from Michigan governor John Swainson as a state workmen's compensation referee. In 1963 Conyers served on the National Lawyers Committee for Civil Rights under Law, a group spearheaded by President John F. Kennedy. He was active as a lawyer in the civil rights movement in the southern states and often represented clients in voter registration cases.

The Michigan government post lasted from 1961 until 1964, at which time Conyers resigned and declared his candidacy for a north-side Detroit US House seat. He defeated future Michigan Secretary of State Richard Austin by forty-four votes in the Democratic primary but was never seriously challenged again in a House election, even though the boundaries of his district were changed several times and extended into Detroit's predominantly white suburbs.

He was elected to represent Michigan's First Congressional District; that was renamed the Fourteenth Congressional District. The district covers all of Highland Park and Hamtramck, as well as large portions of Detroit, Dearborn, and the Downriver communities of Melvindale, Allen Park, Southgate, Riverview, Trenton, Gibraltar, and Grosse Ile.

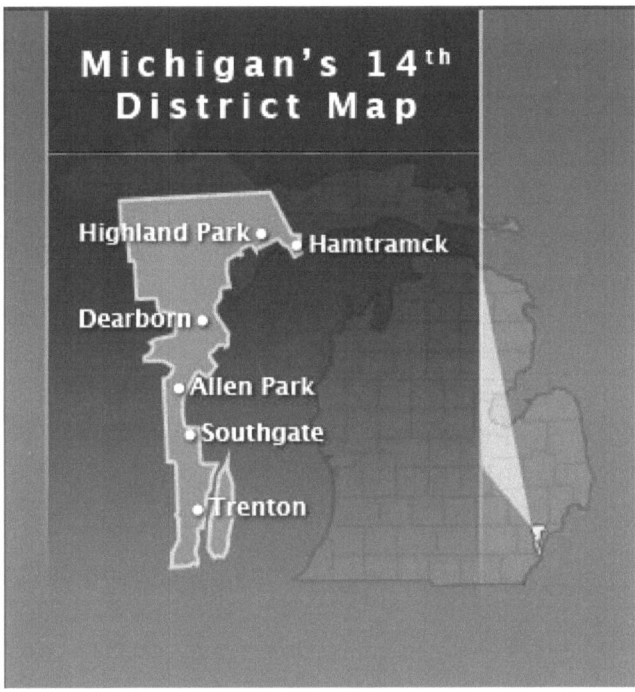

It did not take Conyers long to make his mark legislatively. He signed on as a cosponsor of the landmark Voting Rights Act of 1965, and he backed liberal social legislation including the establishment of the Medicare program, championed by President Lyndon Johnson.

After her arrest, Rosa Parks became an icon of the civil rights movement but suffered hardships as a result. She lost her job at the department store, and her husband quit his job after his boss forbade him from talking about his wife or the legal case. Parks traveled and spoke extensively. In 1957, Raymond and Rosa Parks left Montgomery for Hampton, Virginia, mostly because she was unable to find work. In Hampton, she found a job as a hostess in an inn at black Hampton Institute. Later that year, after the urging of her family, Rosa Parks, her husband Raymond, and her mother, Leona McCauley, moved to Detroit, Michigan.

Ms. Parks worked as a seamstress until 1965, when Conyers hired her as a secretary and receptionist for his congressional office in Detroit. She held this position until she retired in 1988.

US Rep. John Conyers, the Detroit Democrat who is the senior member of the House Judiciary Committee, was elected to Congress in 1964, the year the Civil Rights Act was passed. Parks, whose political views mirrored those of the outspoken Conyers, would remain close to Conyers throughout her life. Conyers recalls the day when Nelson Mandela visited Detroit in 1990. The pair joined the South African leader on stage. Mandela got the crowd to join him in chanting "Rosa Parks!"

Conyers said that day with Mandela caused him to recognize a simple truth: "Rosa Parks is worldwide." Yet the icon was also a warm and generous human being. Thus, when Rosa Parks died, Conyers explained, "America lost a living legend; and I, along with countless others, lost a friend."

As a token of his respect for his former aide's accomplishments, Conyers always referred to her as "Mrs. Parks." But there was nothing formal about their friendship. She regarded him as the most important political leader in the many struggles that she waged— not just for civil rights but for peace, economic justice, and in particular, an end to the death penalty.

The congressman regarded "Mrs. Parks" as something akin to a secular saint, as his warm reflection on her passing makes abundantly clear: "We all knew that Mrs. Parks was frail. We always feared this moment, and now it is here. The extent to which she will be missed cannot be dignified with words. She and her husband moved to Detroit in 1957, and I think it is fair to say we bonded right away. Mrs. Parks was there with me at the beginning of my career as a Congressman in 1965 and worked for me as my administrative assistant for next twenty years. I am therefore one of the lucky few who have had the privilege of being able to call her my colleague as well as my friend."

In 1967 Conyers took the lead in resisting a bill backed by southern conservatives that would have delayed legislative redistricting according to the principle of one person, one vote. After the assassination of the Rev. Martin Luther King Jr. in 1968, Conyers introduced a bill that would designate King's birthday as a national holiday. In 1983, he saw the measure become law. In November of 2012, Conyers will seek his twenty-sixth term in the US House of Representatives.

Having entered the House of Representatives in 1965, Congressman John Conyers is the second most senior member in the House of Representatives. In 1969 Conyers became a founding member of the Congressional Black Caucus and was for many years its senior figure, which is considered the dean of that group. Formed in 1969, the CBC was founded to strengthen African American lawmakers' ability to address the legislative concerns of minority citizens.

In 2006, Congressman Conyers was elected by his congressional colleagues to lead, as chairman, the pivotal House Committee on the Judiciary in the 110th and 111th Congress as well as serve as the chairman of the House Committee on Government Operations (now renamed Committee on Oversight and Government Reform) from 1989 until 1994. In addition to its oversight of the Department of Justice (including the FBI) and the Federal Courts, the Judiciary Committee has jurisdiction over copyright, civil rights, consumer protection, and constitutional issues. Congressman Conyers was also a member of the Judiciary Committee in its 1974 hearings on the Watergate impeachment scandal and played a prominent role in the recent impeachment process, giving him the distinction as the only Judiciary Committee member to have served on both panels and making Nixon's Enemies List. Conyers emerged as a leading black anti-Nixon spokesman.

Identified with social and racial justice issues for the bulk of his career, Conyers has also become involved with various other kinds of legislation. He introduced and worked to bring forward a bill requiring health warning labels on the packaging of alcoholic beverages; the bill became law in 1988. Conyers was one of the first lawmakers to urge a systematic study of the differing treatment blacks and whites received at the hands of police, and the US Department of Justice launched a major national investigation of the issue partly in response to his concerns. Conyers introduced or worked on major legislation dealing with hate crimes, voter registration, and violence against women. On a lighter note, he sponsored legislation that designated a National Tap Dancing Day. "When you ask people about my legislative agenda, it's all over the place," he once said. Conyers continued to rack up huge majorities in his congressional races but lost in two runs for mayor of Detroit. In the 1980s he was a prominent opponent of President Ronald Reagan's strategic defense space-based weapons initiative, commonly known as Star Wars.

In 1998 Conyers participated in his second impeachment proceeding as the House Judiciary Committee took up charges that President Bill Clinton had lied about his involvement with intern

Monica Lewinsky. Though he often wrangled with prosecutor Kenneth Starr, Conyers maintained cordial relationships with Republican House members despite the bitterly partisan atmosphere. Conyers, the senior Democrat on the committee, was the de facto leader of Clinton's defense in the House against impeachment charges.

In 2000 Conyers lent his voice to a growing effort by some African American leaders to raise the issue of reparations that could be paid or otherwise given to African Americans as compensation for the forced expropriation of their labor during the era of slavery and beyond. Laying out the case for reparations, Conyers stressed that the movement was "not coming forward in an accusatory tone toward any citizens or their ancestors," but that "we simply think that Congress should take a look at the lingering effects of slavery so that we may get a deeper appreciation of them and reach some consensus about what the solutions may be. The issue of reparations is not something beyond our understanding," Conyers wrote. "It's a pretty fundamental issue if you look at it. I'm saying it's time we did." In recent years, Mr. Conyers has focused his efforts on promoting economic development in Southeast Michigan, fighting for equal justice and the protection of the civil rights for all Americans, and promoting peace around the world.

Watchdog Reputation: My Brother's Keeper

Conyers has a reputation for keeping a close eye on the activities of his Republican adversaries. That tendency came to life with the US invasion of Iraq in March of 2003, the authorization for which Conyers voted against. Conyers questioned the stated rationale for the war and added his name as plaintiff to a lawsuit contending the war was unconstitutional because it had not been declared by Congress.

In 2005 he gathered 500,000 signatures on an online petition asking President George W. Bush to address the so-called Downing Street memo, a British government document that appeared to suggest that the Bush administration had settled on war with Iraq regardless of the outcome of diplomatic initiatives. "If these disclosures are true," Conyers said at a House committee meeting, "then brave Americans and innocent Iraqis would have lost their lives for a lie."

In 2005 Conyers and Representative Stephanie Tubbs Jones introduced the Voting Opportunity and Technology Enhancement and Rights (VOTER) Act, designed to address voting problems that plagued both the 2002 and 2004 elections and that in the eyes of many observers had an unfair impact on African Americans who were attempting to vote. Conyers also worked on measures to help the impoverished Caribbean nation of Haiti and supported a variety of measures designed to insure that musicians could maintain copyright to their works. Clearly the dean of African American politicians had lost none of his energy as he reached senior citizen status.

Working for the People of Detroit, of the Downriver Communities, and Around the World:

Congressman Conyers is dedicated to improving the lives of the people of the Fourteenth Congressional District. During the 111th Congress, he worked tirelessly to secure funding for deserving groups and organizations. In yet another example of his dedication to the city of Detroit, he secured $2.75 million in funding for various infrastructure improvements, including $750,000 for the restoration of the Detroit Institute of Arts and an additional $500,000 for airport improvements. Reforming the justice system remains at the forefront of his mind, as evident in his ability to secure more than $3 million in funding for justice-related projects. This includes $1 million for a police department firearm reduction initiative, $400,000 for the Wayne County Juvenile Mentoring Program, and $550,000 for the City of Detroit Parolees, Technical Parole Violators, and Former Prisoners Project, which aims at providing former prisoners with job training and employment opportunities.

Creating and Protecting Good Jobs in Southeast Michigan:

Congressman Conyers worked closely with the other members of Michigan's congressional delegation to ensure that the millions of jobs provided by Michigan's auto industry survived the 2008 financial crisis.

Congressman Conyers has also introduced several pieces of legislation aimed providing the currently unemployed with training programs and good jobs. His bill, HR 870, the Humphrey-Hawkins Twenty-First Century Full Employment and Training Act, would create a new tax on Wall Street speculators that would pour billions of dollars a year into Workforce Investment Act (WIA) training programs and innovative public and private sector jobs programs across the country. In the 111th Congress, Mr. Conyers also authored H.R. 4179, the SHARE Credit Act, which would establish a business tax credit that would help prevent layoffs.

Afghanistan and Iraq:

Representative Conyers is the founder of the bipartisan Out of Afghanistan Caucus and a cofounder of the Out of Iraq Caucus. The Out of Afghanistan Caucus serves as an informal bipartisan group of congressional members dedicated to reorienting the US commitment to the Afghan government and its people.

Haiti:

In the 111th Congress, Congressman Conyers worked with Senate Foreign Relations Chairman Sen. John Kerry (D-MA) to propose legislation that would ensure that the United States' response to the tragic earthquake in Haiti was comprehensive, coordinated, and efficient. The Haiti Empowerment, Assistance, and Rebuilding Act of 2010 would establish benchmarks for success and a clear reporting and accountability system for transparency so that Americans know where US foreign aid spending in Haiti is going and whether or not it is achieving its desired impact.

Fighting for Michigan's Working Families:

Michigan's Homeowners:

In the 111th Congress, Congressman Conyers authored HR 1106, the Helping Families Save Their Homes Act. This law would allow bankruptcy court judges to reduce the principal and interest rates for homeowners facing foreclosure and help them remain in their homes. HR 1106 successfully passed the House of Representatives on March 5, 2009, before being filibustered by Senate Republicans.

Protecting Medicare, Medicaid, and Social Security:

In the 111th Congress, Congressman Conyers led an effort in which 133 members of Congress ultimately pledged to oppose any legislative effort to cut Social Security benefits or raise the retirement age. In the 112th Congress, he has authored H. Con. Res. 72, which states that it is the sense of Congress that no deficit reduction plan should cut Medicare, Medicaid, or Social Security benefits.

Providing Leadership on Judiciary Issues:

Representative Conyers has introduced and endorsed legislation to advance civil liberties, ensure equal protection and access to the voting booth, and combat violence against women. Since September 11th, he has worked to strike a balance between keeping our country safe from terrorism and protecting the civil liberties of our citizens. Conyers has supported the administration, proper law enforcement, and intelligence authorities' efforts to prevent terrorism. At the same time, he has worked to make sure that civil liberties and civil rights are preserved in the process.

In response to problems experienced by voters during the 2000 presidential election, Representative Conyers co-authored comprehensive election reform legislation to end discriminatory election practices, which was enacted in October of 2002. This bill advances civil rights and protects voting rights, among other provisions, by establishing federal minimum voting rights standards for election machines and requiring voting sites to be made accessible to those with disabilities.

As an outspoken critic of violence against women, Congressman Conyers was also a lead sponsor of the Violence Against Women Act (VAWA), which was enacted in 1994 and re-authorized in 2001. It provides funding for federal, state, and local programs to combat domestic violence and sexual assault. In addition, Mr. Conyers is the principal author of the End Racial Profiling Act, legislation that would ensure that the rights of all Americans are protected by banning racial profiling nationwide and by requiring all federal, state, and local law enforcement agencies to take administrative steps to eliminate the practice. He also introduced the Hate Crimes Prevention Act, legislation that would place a wide range of hate crimes under federal jurisdiction and allow for enhanced support by the federal government of local investigation and prosecution.

Fighting for Michigan's Working Families:

Representative Conyers has spent his entire career fighting for Michigan's working families. As a supporter of the UAW, Congressman Conyers is well aware of the struggles that affect working families. With families facing skyrocketing health care costs, rising unemployment, and an outdated minimum wage, Conyers continues to fight for equal pay for women and minorities, a raise in the minimum wage, and the full employment of all Americans.

In the 111th Congress, Congressman Conyers authored HR 6436, the State Public Funds Protection Act, which would keep taxpayer dollars out of corporate anti-union campaigns.

Working for Quality, Affordable Health Care:

For more than three decades, Congressman Conyers has led efforts in Congress to reform the health care system. He is the founder of the forty-five-member Congressional Universal Health Care Task Force. The caucus introduced H. Con. Res 99, which was supported by over 450 grassroots organizations across the country and dozens of members of Congress. He recently reintroduced HR 676, the Expanded and Improved Medicare For All Act, a single-payer health insurance bill that has the endorsement of over four thousand physicians nationally. This legislation would guarantee every American access to affordable, comprehensive, quality health care.

Congressman Conyers has authored the Resident Physician Safety Protection Act in order to reduce the hours that resident physicians work so they can perform their work safely. Congressman Conyers's advocacy directly led to a decision by the American Medical Association and the Accreditation Council for Graduate Medical Education to adopt major provisions of the bill.

In the 111th Congress, Congressman Conyers introduced H.R. 2381, the Nurse and Healthcare Worker Protection Act. This legislation would require the secretary of labor to promulgate a rule creating a standard for safe patient handling and injury prevention to prevent musculoskeletal disorders for health care workers handling patients in health care facilities. Under this standard, health facilities would have to purchase an adequate number of mechanical lifting devices for their employees to transport and lift patients.

In the 112th Congress, Congressman Conyers has introduced HR 894, the Maternal Mortality Accountability Act. This legislation would create a national reporting standard and provide resources to the states to encourage the accurate tracking of maternal deaths. HR 894 has been endorsed by the American Congress of Obstetricians and Gynecologists (ACOG), Amnesty International, and the American Medical Student Association (AMSA).

Holding Wall Street Accountable:

During the 111th Congress, Congressman Conyers was selected by his colleagues to sit on the conference committee of the landmark Dodd-Frank Wall Street Reform and Consumer Protection Act of 2011. During the negotiations, Congressman Conyers fought to ensure that the bill protected consumers while maintaining the antitrust powers of the Department of Justice.

Congressman Conyers has also fought to reinstate the so-called Glass-Steagall banking law, which required that traditional banks and investment houses remain separate.

Around the World

International Engagement Fighting for Peace:

In the 111th Congress, Congressman Conyers authored a key provision in the 2011 National Defense Authorization Act, which required the secretaries of defense and state to explore ways the United States could prevent accidental war with Iran.

In the 112th Congress, Mr. Conyers has worked on a bipartisan basis to successfully amend both the 2012 National Defense Authorization Act and the 2012 Defense Appropriations Act to block funding for the deployment of US ground troops and mercenaries in Libya.

People, Place and Things:

Mr. and Mrs. Conyers and their two sons, John III and Carl Edward

Congressional Black Caucasus members

Congressman Conyers and then-Senator Barack Obama

Congressman Conyers with his love of musical instrument

President Barack Obama signs the Fraud Enforcement and Recovery Act into law as Rep. John Larson (D-CT) (2nd R), Senate Democratic Leader Sen. Harry Reid (D-NV) (3rd R), and Rep. John Conyers (D-MI) (4th R) look on during a ceremony in the East Room of the White House, May 20, 2009, in Washington, DC.

President Barack Obama (R) shakes hands with Rep. John Conyers (D-MI) (L) during an event to host recipients of National Association of Police Organizations' (NAPO) Top Cops Awards at the Rose Garden of the White House, May 12, 2009, in Washington, DC.

Rep. John Conyers (D-MI) speaks during day two of the Democratic National Convention (DNC) at the Pepsi Center, August 26, 2008, in Denver, Colorado. Sen. Barack Obama (D-IL) will be officially be nominated as the Democratic candidate for US president on the last day of the four-day convention.

References:

John Conyers, DAAHP (The Detroit African-American History Project), http://www.daahp.wayne.edu/biographiesDisplay.asp?id=75 (December 12, 2005).

John Conyers Jr.'s Biography, Congressman John Conyers Jr. web-page, http://www.house.gov/conyers (December 12, 2005).